Pageant Wagon Radio Drama

PRESENTS

The Adventures of Marshall Mission

Christmas Takes a Holiday

DIRECTOR'S SCRIPT

Written by Kathryn Ross

A Pageant Wagon Radio Drama
The Adventures of Marshall Mission: Christmas Takes a Holiday
Director's Script
Written by Kathryn Ross

Pageant Wagon Publishing
A Division of Pageant Wagon Productions LLC

ISBN: 978-0-9910070-9-7

A Pageant Wagon Radio Drama
The Adventures of Marshall Mission: "Christmas Takes a Holiday"

First Performed December 4, 2009

Cast:

3 male
3 female
3 male or female

Original Cast of Characters:

Announcer/Director, Cymbal..Amaris Beamer
Wilhelmina Weather, Keyboard....................................Cassidy Weyman
Marshall Mission..Dawson Coyle
Brillo Boy..Sean McLoone
Hustle, Flute...Jordan Vasquez
Bustle, Trimbal...Larissa Ippolito
Miss Frieda, Charlie..Hope Miller
Ebenezer Frenzy, Larry..Jack Markley
Moe, Sound Engineer...Wiley Markley

Setting:

The clock turns back with a vintage/retro atmosphere, circa 1930's/1940's radio station. Live broadcasts featured dramatic presentations employing the talents of an actor's voice and various sound effects. Stories come to life in the imagination of listeners.

SET

Long table set center on a 1' high platform stage with shorter table set in "L" shape, right. At left on main table is keyboard and music. The rest of the table space has all the various props, etc. for sound effects. The prop list is available online via FREE download printable with other production notes at www.pageantwagonpublishing.com/marshall-mission-christmas. The smaller table has an array of hats to be won by various characters –most especially by the Sound Engineer and Wilhelmina who change hats according to the sound effect and script. Christmas trees for decorating are set to stage left and right.

A microphone is set on the table for the Sound Engineer. Down Stage Left and Down Stage Right microphones are set on stands. Music stands are set in front of each microphone with a full script in binders. Actors use the scripts to assist with lines and cues, but must be well schooled in the delivery and timing of lines, and characterizations.

Three chairs each are set facing the audience, but behind the microphones and music stand with scripts. Prop hats for each character are under the chairs for quick change. Refer to the Production Notes online. One chair is set Stage Left side on an angle. Two Stools are behind sound effects table. Seats are assigned thus:

> Slanted Stage Left Chair: Announcer/Director
> Behind Sound Effects Table: Moe and Wilhelmina
> Stage Right Chairs (L-R): Marshall Mission, Miss Frieda, Brillo Boy
> Stage Left Chairs (L-R): Hustle, Frenzy, Bustle

Note: *The cast may refer to themselves by their first names throughout the play unless they are acting a role in the radio drama. The names of the original cast are retained in this script in some parts for ease of reading. Once you have cast your production, have them make the appropriate changes in the script to their names, or you may simply use the original cast names if that is easier.*

OPENING:
DECK THE HALLS Music up – (use a Soundtrax or perform a capella; you may omit the lyrics and just open with Christmas music instrumentals. See download production notes for more details on the musical elements of the show including sheet music for the original commercial jingles.)

Players enter in small groups, setting up props and scripts and decorations. Narrator is center stage, directing all the action—some basic blocking is provided here in the Prologue, but very scant directions are included elsewhere.

All: Deck the Halls with boughs of holly
Fa la la la la la la la
Tis the season to be jolly
Fa la la la la la la la *(continue humming tune low)*

Hope: *(X center to Amaris carrying decoration)* I'm so excited about our Radio Theatre Show tonight! *(X to SL to decorate tree)*

Amaris: Me, too! We've worked so hard to get just the right old-time radio atmosphere.

Cassidy: The keyboard is hooked up and ready to go!

Amaris: With a little help from a few modern tech instruments. *(Jordan & Larissa X to Cassidy with script—mime asking question about music)*

Wiley: All my hats and sound effect props are ready!

Amaris: Check!

All: All the props and costumes set to stage right.
Fa la la la la la la la la
Get your scripts all ready for a really big night!
Fa la la la la la la la la
We've rehearsed our parts and learned our lines
We expect to have a jolly great time!
It's a Radio Theatre Holiday Review
For a very Merry Christmas to all of you!

Jordan: *(X to Amaris with Jordan, Cassidy, & script)* Say, do we all sing at this spot?

Amaris: *(checks script)* Yep—we all sing that line together.

Larissa: And listen, we've been working on our evil laugh! *(Jordan & Larissa evil laugh)*

Cassidy: Sounds like some foul weather ahead!

Amaris: Check! *(Cassidy returns to keyboard, Larissa & Jordan help Hope decorate tree SL)*

Dawson & Sean: *(X to Amaris, saluting)* Marshall Mission and Brillo Boy reporting for duty!

Amaris: Our heroes! Are you ready to save Christmas?

Jack: *(X from SR tree pushing between Sean & Dawson)* Not if I can help it!

Hope: *(Pretends to be afraid; stands L of Amaris)* Oh, no! Not that villain again!

Wiley: Hey you guys—which hat should I start off with?

Dawson: It doesn't matter—this is radio theatre.

Sean: But, we have a studio audience!

Jack: Wear the Santa hat.

Wiley: Nah, I'll go with the reindeer antlers.

Amaris: Whatever. Quick—we've got to start!

All: Deck the Halls with boughs of holly
Fa la la la la la la la la
Tis the season to be jolly
Fa la la la la la la la la
We've rehearsed our parts and learned our lines
We expect to have a jolly great time!
It's a Radio Theatre Holiday Review
For a very Merry Christmas to all of you!
A very Merry Christmas to all of you!

NOTE: *At the end of the song, the cast makes a formation like the end of a dance production number. From these starting positions, block the following backstory introductory lines, allowing the cast to casually move about the stage speaking directly to the audience, to make it more interesting.*

Hope: Almost two hundred years ago, Michael Faraday and Joseph Henry had an idea!

Dawson: They thought that an electrical current flowing in one wire could produce a current in a second wire, even if the two wires were not touching.

Jordan: They believed a wireless connection of electrical energy was possible.

Jack: In the 1890's, Guglielmo Marconi sent the first wireless radio message across the English Channel.

Larissa: Soon, he had placed wireless radio sets in lighthouses all along the coast of England to send and receive Morse code during emergencies at sea.

Cassidy: The first wireless transmission of the human voice happened in 1906 when Reginald Fessenden spoke by radio from Brant Rock, Massachusetts, to ships in the Atlantic Ocean on Christmas Eve.

Amaris: Fessenden read from the Bible and a musician played a violin solo of sacred music. Afterward, listeners were invited to tune in next week at the same time for another broadcast program.

Wiley: But, it wasn't until after World War I that radio became a normal part of American households.

Jordan: In 1922, less than 60,000 families owned radios.

Hope: But, by 1930, only eight years later, over 13 million families owned a radio, connected to the world at large. The information age, as we know it today, was born.

Dawson: Radio programs used sound effects and scripts to make their broadcasts seem real, painting detailed pictures in the imaginations of their listeners.

Cassidy: The arts, music, drama, comedy, live news coverage, and intelligent conversation filled the airwaves.

Sean: Radio theatres reached their greatest popularity in the 1930's and 1940's.

Amaris: In the big broadcasting stations, theatrical stars performed on the radio in front of live studio audiences.

Jack: Signs flashed telling everyone when they were broadcasting "ON THE AIR".

Wiley: And when they should applaud. *(hold up applause sign and all applaud)*

Larissa: The radio theatre stage was full of cumbersome technical equipment and large microphones.

Cassidy: Actors read from a script and didn't need to wear costumes. Though, for the studio audience, they might use a special hat or prop in fun.

Sean: When actors weren't reading their lines in front of the microphone, they'd sit in a chair and wait for their cue.

Dawson: Special Sound Engineers were in charge of creating all the sound effects needed to tell the stories. *(Wiley makes all sorts of strange sounds with his props)* There were clever ways of making all sorts of sounds.

Hope: Different shows were broadcast with commercial sponsors advertising their products. Educational shows and sporting events were popular . . .

Jordan: . . . and many programs featured Christian preachers teaching about the Bible and faith in God.

Amaris: Family entertainment was very popular—adventure stories, mystery stories, comedy shows, and the exciting serial stories told in short episodes, leaving you with a cliffhanger ending.

Jack: You'd have to wait until the next episode was broadcast the following week at the same time—or perhaps later on in the day—before you could find out what happened next.

All: You wouldn't want to miss that!

Wiley: Musicians played instruments in the studio—whole orchestras—and famous singing stars visited, performing their hit songs live and in person.

Larissa: Radio became the common experience uniting millions of Americans—all classes of society and every ethnic group listened to radio.

Dawson: Live broadcasts of important world events and instant access to information made Americans participants in history rather than just observers of history.

Amaris: Tonight, we're turning back the clock to make history alive again, recreating our own broadcast of a vintage Radio Theatre Show.

Cassidy: And, since it's the holiday season, why not a Christmas show!

Amaris: Just like one hundred years ago, in 1906, during that very first radio transmission of the human voice, when Mr. Fessenden broadcast Bible readings and praise music to ships at sea on Christmas Eve . . .

Jordan: We can do the same thing!

Sean: A Christmas cliffhanger serial adventure!

Jack: With commercial advertisements!

Hope: And music!

Wiley: Don't forget the sound effects!

Cassidy: And maybe even a weather report!

Amaris: Places everyone! WPWP Radio Theatre is on-the-air!

(All take places for opening – Music up for WPWP RADIO THEME)

Announcer: Good evening, ladies and gentlemen! You are listening to WPWP Wireless Broadcast Radio. We welcome you, our studio and listening audience, as we begin yet another broadcast day brought to you by our good friends at Heavenly House Coffee and the Manna Mix Baking Company.

(Trimbal, Flute, and Cymbal move to L mic; Music cue up—HEAVENLY HOUSE COFFEE theme)

(Doorbell ring)

Trimbal: Welcome to the Heavenly House! Mmmmm! Smell that aroma! A sweet smelling aroma—pleasing to the Lord—would you like a cup?

(Sound of coffee pouring)

(Sound of drink slurping)

Flute: Mmmmm . . . delicious! Full, abundant, and flavorful!

Cymbal: What else would you expect from . . .

Trio: . . . the Biblical Blend.

(Sound of drink slurping)

Trimbal: Ahhh! My cup runneth over . . .

Flute: Surely goodness and mercy will follow . . .

Cymbal: All the days of my life . . .

Trimbal: And I will dwell in Heavenly House Coffee forever!

Trio: *(sing)* AHHH! Heavenly House Coffee—the Biblical Blend!

(Doorbell ring)

(Music up for MANNA MIX THEME)

Announcer: And what better way to serve a delicious cup of hot Heavenly House Coffee, than with your favorite breads and dessert cakes from the Manna Mix Baking Company!

Trio: *(sing)* Taste and see that the Lord is good!
Taste and see that the Lord is good!
Taste and see that the Lord is good!
Manna Mix! For all your baking needs!
Mmmm Mmmm—The Lord is good!

Announcer: Yes, bread from heaven is made available for one and all! Manna Mix Baking Company provides a full line of baking products for the whole family!

Trimbal: Breads, muffins, pastries, pies,

Flute: Cookies, cakes, in every size!

Trimbal: Anoint with some oil and sweeten with honey,

Flute: You'll be fed to the full and get more for your money!

Trio: *(sing)* Taste and see that the Lord is good,
Manna Mix! For all your baking needs,
Mmmm Mmmm—The Lord is good!

(Music up for WEATHER THEME)

Announcer: Do you hear that tune? It's time for the weather with our own WPWP forecaster, Wilhelmina Weather!

(Music for WEATHER fades – Wilhelmina puts on fur hat – X to L mic)

Wilhelmina: And this IS Wilhelmina Weather here with your own local forecast for a vicinity near you! High winds possible, and sunny skies probable as morning moves to the afternoon, and the cloud covering continues bringing blue skies and stifling hot temperatures throughout area. By sunset snow accumulation is expected to reach the 3 foot marker in the lowlands and may settle to a record 6 inches in the higher elevations. Chance of rain is 100 percent. Precipitation 20. Humidity at 98. Looks like a dry and dusty one this holiday season. Break out the blankets, you'll need them tonight. Overnight lows will be in the high '80's. Overall, it's a most unusual day!

(Music for WEATHER up)

This is Wilhelmina Weather with your own local forecast for a vicinity near you! I'll be back later in the broadcast with another weather update for your WPWP day!

Announcer: And now, it's time for another exciting episode of, "The Adventures of Marshall Mission!"

(FANFARE—applause)

Larissa: Brought to you today by your friends at the Manna Mix Baking Company—and Heavenly House Coffee, the Biblical Blend!

Jordan: Taste and see that the Lord is good.

Hope: And all your friends at Toytown! Take the hustle and bustle out of your holiday shopping at Toytown—your one stop shop for all things Marshall Mission!

(MARSHALL MISSION THEME music cue up)

Cast: *(sung)* His name is Marshall
Janitor on a mission
He almost never gets paid

And he doesn't make commission.
He's just a saint
He'll fill your heart with hope.
He fights the bad guys
With his secret soap on a rope!
His name is Marshall
And this is his song.
His call is clear
He rids the world
Of dirt and of wrong!
Marshall - Marshall Mission
Marshall - Marshall Mission!

(Music cut to SECRET AGENT THEME music)

Announcer: Marshall Mission, Janitor Man,

(Dawson puts on Janitor Man hat and steps to microphone)

with his secret store of cleaning supplies, not only makes your floors and windows sparkle, but he has the power to eliminate the stain of sin from the human heart, as well. With his faithful assistant, Brillo Boy,

(Sean puts on Brillo Boy hat and steps to microphone)

and an arsenal of cleansers, detergents, polishing waxes, and his most secret weapon of all—the soap on a rope collection—Marshall Mission travels the world wide in search of wrongs to right, dirt to vacuum, and filthy rags to wash whiter than snow.

(Pause–O LITTLE TOWN OF BETHLEHEM music cue)

It is the holiday season and today we find Marshall Mission and Brillo Boy trimming their humble apartment abode with a smattering of tasteful festive decor. A peaceful scene, for the moment . . .

(Music OMINOUS CHORD then fade)

Marshall: Hmmmm, what's this I smell? A sweet aroma? A pure delight to the senses! Why . . . it's coming from the kitchen!

(Dinner bell rings)

Brillo Boy: Christmas treats are served, O, noble, noble Master of Mops!

Marshall: Brillo Boy! My faithful friend and promising apprentice! You've Been baking! Smells delectable! What is that sumptuous scent?

Brillo Boy: Why, it's just your favorite food and drink in the whole wide of the world!

Marshall: Pizza and Coke?

Brillo Boy: NO! It's my own secret Christmas cookie recipe made with the fresh flours, powders, and spices from the Manna Mix Baking Company! Served up, just as you like, with a nice warm mug of skim milk!

(Sound of cookie eating and milk drinking)

Marshall: Mmmmm! Could there be anything more satisfying? Why, this is angel's food direct from heaven!

Brillo Boy: Manna Mix for all your holiday baking needs! Taste and see . . .

(More food chewing and drink slurping)

Marshall: Ah, yes! The Lord is good! So, Brillo Boy, what den of iniquity am I off to cleanse and purify today! An oil spill in Alaska? A hurricane aftermath in the Gulf of Mexico? More scum and villainy in the hallowed halls of human government?

Brillo Boy: No chief. Not today. Only Miss Frieda from across the hall. She seems to be having an organizational problem with her holiday planning. She left this note scribbled on a crumpled piece of wrapping paper under our door this morning!

(Crumple paper sound)

Marshall Mission: Hmmm . . . scribbles . . . crumples . . . not good. Not good at all. Why, it says here she fears . . . *(OMINOUS CHORDS)* . . . she may be falling victim to . . . the holiday "frenzy."

Brillo Boy: Eureka Vacuums, Marshall Mission! Do you think it's serious?

Marshall Mission: When "frenzy's" afoot, it's always serious. *(pause)* Brillo Boy, grab the Dust Buster and let us—be off!

(Sound rattling and a door slamming shut)

Announcer: No sooner had our hero and his faithful apprentice found their way across the hall to Miss Frieda's apartment door, but that a pungent odor was swiftly detected . . .

Brillo Boy: Eureka Vacuums! What's that nasty smell, Marshall Mission?

Marshall: Brillo Boy! I know that smell! That pungent odor you so swiftly detected—it is . . . it is . . . quick! We must bust down the door! Filth and Foul are afoot!

(Sound of running feet and door being "busted open")

(Sound of four feet slapping the floor)

(Sound of Christmas music screeching on a broken record)

Brillo Boy: Ick & Yick! That awful smell is stronger! And where's that horrible noise coming from? Poor Miss Frieda! And . . . and . . . just look at the mess in here!

(Sound of rustling through a "mess" by scrunching wrapping paper)

Marshall: Oh, Miss Frieda! What have you gotten yourself into. Look! We are knee deep in wrapping paper, ribbons, gaudy flashing lights and Santa Clauses!

Brillo Boy: Where's that harsh red glow coming from? Oh, look, there!

Marshall: Of course . . . to be expected . . . it's Rudolph the Red-Nosed Reindeer.

Brillo Boy: How can we stop that broken record, Marshall Mission?!

Marshall: Find the stereo phonograph, of course!

(Sound of tripping and falling)

Marshall: OUCH!

Brillo Boy: Marshall Mission! Are you alright?

Marshall: Certainly! Just my keen senses detecting the whereabouts of that . . . ah HA!

(Broken record sound stops)

Brillo Boy: Whew! That's better! But the smell!

Marshall: Here! In the kitchen!

Brillo Boy: Burnt Christmas cookies!

Marshall: What a dastardly waste of Manna Mix Baking flour, powders, and spices.

Brillo Boy: And Miss Frieda is nowhere to be found!

(Sound of a "bang")

Marshall: What was that?

Brillo Boy: It's Miss Frieda! *(calling)* Miss Frieda!! Miss Frieda!! It's me, that nice Brillo Boy from across the hall!

Marshall: SHHH! Be Quiet! Listen!

(Sound of banging)

Marshall: Quick, Brillo Boy! To the closet!

(Sound of rustling through stuff)

Marshall: Alright! The gig is up! It is I, Marshall Mission, Janitor Man! That brave defender of greaseless countertops and dust free windowsills! You are surrounded! Come out with your hands up!

(Sound of door creaking open and OMINOUS CHORDS)

Hustle & Bustle: *(madly laughing)*

Hustle: Greaseless countertops!

Bustle: Dust-free windowsills!

Hustle & Bustle: Not when WE move in!!

Brillo Boy: EEWWW! Marshall Mission! I've never seen such a confused mess before!

Hustle: Confused???

Bustle: Mess???

Hustle & Bustle: *(madly laughing – sing-song)* We're such a confused mess!!

Hustle: What a nice thing to say . . .

Bustle: . . . and we hardly know you!

Brillo Boy: Marshall Mission, what can this mean?!

Marshall: I should have known you were here the moment I saw your signature in all this clutter! Hustle & Bustle—hiding in a closet! How typical!

Hustle & Bustle: *(mad laugh)*

Brillo Boy: You mean—THE Hustle & THE Bustle . . . of the Holiday Season???

Hustle & Bustle: *(sing to "Deck the Halls" tune)* 'Tis the season to be too busy—

Marshall: Not just the "holiday" season, Brillo Boy. Anytime of the year these two vile minions can disrupt peace and tranquility with their assault weapons of clutter, chaos, and confusion.

Hustle: *(mocking)* Clutter . . . chaos . . .

Bustle: *(mocking)* . . . and confusion!

Hustle & Bustle: *(singing to "My Favorite Things" tune)* These are a few of our favorite things!!!!

Marshall: Silence! Criminals! What have you done with Miss Frieda!?

Hustle: We did nothing!

Bustle: She did it all by herself!

Hustle: She's the one who didn't make any lists . . .

Bustle: . . . or check them twice.

Hustle: She's the one who spent too much money on too much STUFF!

Bustle: Running from this store to that sale . . .

Hustle: Stringing flashy lights from here to there . . .

Bustle: Getting wound up in wrapping . . .

Hustle: . . .and tied up in bows . . .

Bustle: . . . and now she can't tell . . .

Hustle: . . . her head from her toes!!

Hustle & Bustle: *(mad laugh)*

Marshall: You brutes!

Brillo Boy: But, what of Miss Frieda!?

Marshall: Isn't it obvious, Brillo Boy! Poor Miss Frieda has gotten caught up in the Hustle and Bustle of the holiday season—Oh! The madness of the world and its woes! She has been carried away—

Brillo Boy: No, Marshall Mission! Not Miss Frieda!

Marshall: I'm afraid so, Brillo Boy. She had been carried away—in a FRENZY!

(OMINOUS CHORDS)

Brillo Boy: Oh, Marshall Mission! We must save her!

Marshall Mission: We will! And we'll start right here! Brillo Boy—the Dust Buster! Take this Hustle & Bustle!

(SECRET AGENT THEME music up; sound of Dust Buster)

Hustle & Bustle: *(wildly screaming)* NO! NO! Not the Dust Buster!!!!

(Music & dust buster build to loud climax, then cut—sharp silence and pause)

Brillo Boy: They're gone! They've disappeared! Along with all the wrapping paper and ribbons, and flashing lights, and gaudy Santas, and . . . even Rudolph! All gone!

Marshall: Yes, but, they'll be back. They always come back.

Brillo Boy: Poor Miss Frieda! If she has gotten caught up in Hustle and Bustle and carried away in a Frenzy, how will she ever be able to celebrate the true freedom the Christmas season means for her—for the world!?

Marshall: There is only one way, Brillo Boy. Dust Busting the disorder in her apartment is one thing, but now we must rescue her from the clutches of Frenzy and clean up the clutter, chaos, and confusion of Hustle and Bustle in her mind and heart.

Brillo Boy: Holy Windex, Marshall Mission!

Marshall: This is no easy task, for she is not in the hands of just any Frenzy.

Brillo Boy: No, Marshall Mission, no! Not Miss Frieda!

Marshall: It's true. Miss Frieda is now a prisoner of . . .

(OMINOUS CHORDS)

Marshall: His Most High Grinchness—Ebenezer Frenzy!!!!

(OMINOUS CHORDS)

Announcer: Will Marshall Mission and Brillo Boy find poor, confused Miss Frieda? Will she ever be able to bake edible Christmas cookies again? Will Hustle and Bustle find another closet to hide in? And just who is this villain, His Most High Grinchness, Ebenezer Frenzy? Is there a cleanser in Marshall Mission's arsenal strong enough to mop up this chaotic clutter of a hot mess and set Miss Frieda clean free? For the answers to these and other questions, tune in next time for the continuing adventures of Marshall Mission, Janitor Man!!

(MARSHALL MISSION THEME music up)

Cast: His name is Marshall
And this is his song
His call is clear
He rids the world
Of dirt and of wrong.
Marshall - Marshall Mission
Marshall - Marshall Mission

(Larry, Moe, & Charlie put on silly hats and remain at microphones—others sit.)

Larry: *(in sing-song, mimicking the Three Stooges)* Hello . . .

Moe: Hello . . .

Charlie: Hello . . .

All Three: Hello!

Larry: Say—where'd you get that nifty tee-shirt!?

Moe: Where'd you get that keen lunchbox!?

Larry & Moe: Eureka Vacuums! Where'd you get that Marshall Mission Action Figure!!

Charlie: The same place YOU can get all this and more! Take a trip to Toytown!

All Three: Toytown! WOW!

(TOYTOWN music up)

Charlie: At Toytown you'll find the latest in Marshall Mission Toys!

Larry: Look! Marshall Mission's dust buster really busts dust!

Moe: Cool! This Scrubbing Bubbles Super Soaker is the Bomb!

Charlie: And don't forget all the exciting action figures of your favorite heroes! See! Brillo Boy's Brillo hair works wonders on mom's stainless steel sink!

Larry & Moe: Ooooooo!

Charlie: And for the little ones—bath time is really clean fun with . . .

Larry & Moe: Marshall Mission's Sponge-o-Matic!

Charlie: Just drop the Sponge-o-Matic capsules into the bath water and watch them turn into . . .

Moe: . . . giant Marshall Mission bath sponges! Right before your very eyes! Squeeze and squirt the secret soap solution and it's grime-be-gone in the bathtub!!

Larry: Say! What about something for Dad!?

Charlie: Put Dad on the top of your Christmas gift list always with . . .

Larry & Moe: Marshall Mission's Soap-on-a-Rope!! Hurray!!

Moe: And Mom, enjoy spending time with your children reading aloud from Marshall Mission's Free & Clean Adventure Series—stories your children will love and household cleaning tips you'll use again and again!

Charlie: But wait! There's more! Pencils! Jewelry! Wash-buckets! Mops! Baked beans and microwaves—the fun never stops!

Larry: And introducing . . .

All Three: The Marshall Mission Janitor Man Game!

Larry: So easy to play!

Moe: Just swing your rope . . .

Charlie: . . . and throw your soap!

Larry: Be the first to capture and clean that grime boss himself—that Bah Humbug—Ebenezer Frenzy—and you're the WINNER!

Charlie: And where do we go to get all this neat-o stuff???

All Three: TOYTOWN

Charlie: Look for the Toytown nearest you, today!!

(TOYTOWN music ends—Larry, Moe, & Charlie return to places and remove hats.)

Announcer: That's "The Adventures of Marshall Mission" brought to you today by your friends at Toytown, carrying the complete line of Marshall Mission Action Figures, games and toys! Pencils, jewelry, wash-buckets, mops, baked beans and microwaves—the fun never stops! Marshall Mission—at a Toytown near you!

(WEATHER Music up)

And now - time for the weather with our own WPWP forecaster, Wilhelmina Weather!

(Wilhelmina puts on Sun Hat with large Sun Glasses and steps to microphone; Music for WEATHER fades)

Wilhelmina: And it IS Wilhelmina Weather here with your own local forecast for a vicinity near you! Those high winds have diminished due to a low front in the northeast moving against the jet stream flowing southwest so you can expect to feel that arctic chill throughout the upper basin of the country's mid-section. The barometer has fallen in the mountain regions as a low hanging fog has moved into the gulf with wave heights of close to 4 feet. Surfs-up for you Kansas residents so resin up those snowboards and hit the beach! Looks like clear travel weather across most of the nation with only a 98 percent chance of severe thunderstorms humidity is 25 and the precipitation near 0 with a hot and muggy wind chill factor of minus three! Wow! We're setting some records in Miami with that reading! Overnight lows in the 80's – hope you've got plenty of firewood handy 'cause it looks like a scorcher is on the way for tomorrow. Overall, it's a most unusual day!

(Music for WEATHER up)

This is Wilhelmina Weather with your own local forecast for a vicinity near you! I'll be back later in the broadcast with another informative weather update and wise word for your WPWP day!

Announcer: Coming up— "The Adventures of Marshall Mission–Christmas Takes a Holiday" Episode 2!

(OMINOUS CHORDS)

When we last left our heroes, Marshall Mission, Janitor Man, and his faithful assistant, Brillo Boy, successfully battled the confused mess of Hustle and Bustle that had invaded the normally clear thinking, spic-n-span existence of their good neighbor, Miss Frieda from across the hall. But, the damage was already done. Miss Frieda, having been caught up in Hustle and Bustle, was now carried away in Frenzy—His Most High Grinchness, Ebenezer Frenzy—and was being held prisoner in Frenzy Fortress, doomed to a holiday season of busyness and confusion with the promise of more to come in the new year. Is there any rest for the weary? Will she ever be able to freely share and celebrate the true reason for the season of "Peace on earth, good will towards men?" In peace?

(MARSHALL MISSION THEME music up)

Cast: *(sing)*

His name is Marshall
Janitor on a mission
He almost never gets paid
He doesn't make commission.
He's just a saint
He'll fill your heart with hope.
He fights the bad guys
With his secret soap-on-a-rope.

His name is Marshall
And this is his song

His call is clear
He rids the world
Of dirt and of wrong
Marshall - Marshall Mission
Marshall - Marshall Mission

Announcer: As our story continues, Marshall Mission, Janitor Man, and Brillo Boy, follow the messy footprints of their sworn enemy of all things foul. Hopefully Hustle and Bustle will leave a trail that can lead them straight to His Most High Grinchness, Ebenezer Frenzy—where it is feared poor Miss Frieda is locked away in his Frenzy Fortress, running in confused circles with Fear and Anxiety feeding her in the Dungeon of Despair. And now, Episode 2 titled: "Choo-Choo Clues."

Brillo Boy: Hoover Mover, Marshall Mission! It sure is lucky we found these footprints left by Hustle and Bustle!

Marshall Mission: No luck about it, Brillo Boy. It is positively Providential!

Brillo Boy: But, it seems like we've been following them for a long time. Have we been going in circles? When will it all end?

Marshall Mission: Precisely the questions that Miss Frieda is asking right now! She has been *caught up* in Hustle and Bustle. We're just following in their wake. We must keep our wits about us and never waver in our focus or we may trip and get caught up too. Remember, the heart of Christmas has nothing to do with busy, buying, and bemoaning worldly woes . . . while running to and fro. Eureka!!

Brillo Boy: Vacuums! What have you found, Marshall Mission!?

Marshall: The footprints! They end here at the entrance to this mysterious cave. We must venture forth with caution! We must be near to the enemy's lair. Hustle and Bustle may have called for back-up. Filth and Foul may be afoot! They are ever roaming about seeking whom they may devour. Have your anti-bacterial liquid soap nozzle set on super-suds!

Brillo Boy: Check, Chief!

(Sound of gun being cocked)

Marshall: Ebenezer Frenzy, get ready to eat my suds!!

Brillo Boy: Marshall Mission! What's that sticky, black slop all over the walls of the cave?

Marshall: Hmmm . . . looks like . . . soot. Smoky . . . smutty soot . . .

(Soft sound of train whistle)

Brillo Boy: And that sound . . .

Marshall: What sound?

(Train whistle a bit louder)

Brillo Boy: That sound! Could that be Hustle and Bustle making scummy Christmas music mockingly?

Marshall: Perhaps! It may be a clever ploy to try to confuse us! Focus! Focus!

(Train whistle louder)

Brillo Boy: It sounds so mournful! Maybe it's Miss Frieda crying!

Marshall: If it is, I am well prepared with plenty of Kleenex tissues to whisk away those tear stains!

(Train whistle louder)

(Train engine sound effect)

Brillo Boy: What's *that* fearful sound?? A wild beast? A renegade reindeer??

Marshall: Beastly vermin! It sounds like a vicious growling. Base . . . vulgar . . . getting louder . . . and louder . . .

(Train whistle louder)

Brillo Boy: And poor Miss Frieda! There she goes crying out again!

Marshall: Oh! The inhumanity!

(Train whistle and train engine louder—wave flashlight back and forth at audience)

Brillo Boy: Eureka Vacuums! Marshall Mission! Look! A light! A bright light! And it's coming right for us!! Could it be Rudolph again? But, it's not a red light . . .

Marshall: Of course! Just as I suspected!

(Train whistle and engine loud)

Brillo Boy: Marshall Mission! This isn't a cave! It's a train tunnel! And that's no wild beast! That's a train! We'll be train track tortillas in no time!!

Marshall: Don't panic, Brillo Boy! It's a train all right! It's the Frenzy Express!! Quick! Jump onboard!

Brillo Boy: You mean—

Marshall: Jump! Brillo Boy! Jump! We'll ride the Frenzy Express to the very walls of the Frenzy Fortress where Miss Frieda is a confused prisoner! And there we'll set her clean free!

Marshall & Brillo Boy: FRENZY AWAY!!!

(Train whistle and engine very loud than sudden stop, silent, pause)

Announcer: Will Marshall Mission and Brillo Boy make it safely to the foul Frenzy Fortress where Miss Frieda is imprisoned, running about on a holiday season treadmill that seems unending? How will they make the walls of the fortress come tumbling down so that Miss Frieda can be free to share and enjoy the true spirit of the Christmas season? Will they use Clorox or Pine Sol to scrub a clean place to sit on the train? And what of His Most High Grinchness, Ebenezer Frenzy? What kind of Scrooge could they be up against here!? Tune in next time for the exciting conclusion of "The Adventures of Marshall Mission!"

(MARSHALL MISSION THEME music up)

Cast: His name is Marshall
And this is his song!

His call is clear
He rids the world
Of dirt and of wrong
Marshall - Marshall Mission
Marshall - Marshall Mission

(Doorbell ring)

(HEAVENLY HOUSE COFFEE THEME up—Trimbal, Flute, & Cymbal move to microphones)

Trimbal: I've put the pot on! It'll be Biblical Blend coming right up!

Flute: Biblical Blend! You use Heavenly House Coffee?

Trimbal: Is there really any other?

Cymbal: Not in my cup there won't be! It's Heavenly House, at my house, every day!

Trimbal: Now that's the way to start your morning!

Flute: Well, here's my cup! I'm ready when it's ready!

Cymbal: And it's always ready, fresh and hot! Nothing lukewarm here! Fill my cup, too!

Trimbal: Coming right up!

(Sound of coffee pouring)

(Sound of sipping)

Flute: Mmmm! So satisfying! What a lifesaver!

Cymbal: It's sufficient for me!

Trio: Ahhh! *(sing)* Heavenly House Coffee—The Biblical Blend!

(WEATHER music up)

Announcer: And now for another accu-forecast by our own Wilhelmina Weather!

(Wilhelmina puts on umbrella hat; walks to microphone; WEATHER theme fade)

Wilhelmina: And this IS Wilhelmina Weather with another up to the minute accurate weather forecast for a vicinity near you. Temperatures will be dropping steadily as the sun rises to the high today of 76 degrees in the north and a scorching 45 in the south. Break out the boots and galoshes—it'll be wet and slick out there under those clear skies in the mountains. Traveling looks great along the coastline but bring plenty of anti-freeze for highway safety in the tropic zones. Snow accumulation is expected to be minimal for this time of week and it looks like smooth sailing for you ships at sea with storm warnings throughout the northern seaboard. Overall temperatures make for a delightful summer day in December. As far as I can see, it's just a most unusual day.

(Music for WEATHER)

This is Wilhelmina Weather with your own local forecast for a vicinity near you! I'll be back later for a final wrap-up of the weather and a wise word for your WPWP day!

(MANNA MIX music up—Trimbal, Flute, & Cymbal move to microphone)

Cymbal: And on this most unusual day, don't forget to enjoy your daily cup of Heavenly House Coffee with a bakery favorite from the Manna Mix Baking Company!

Trio: *(sing)* Taste and see that the Lord is good!
Taste and see that the Lord is good!
Taste and see that the Lord is good!
Mmmm Mmmmm! The Lord is good!

Announcer: That's Heavenly House Coffee, The Biblical Blend, and the Manna Mix Baking Company, proud sponsors of quality programming here at WPWP Wireless Radio.

(HEAVENLY HOUSE COFFEE theme up)

Cymbal: No CUP too BIG to hold the BIG flavor and satisfying taste of Heavenly House Coffee—The Biblical Blend!

Trimbal: Fill my BIG cup right now with that luscious liquid Heaven scent!

Flute: Here you go! Coming right up! It's all you need with your daily bread.

(Sound of coffee pouring)

(Sound of slurping sip)

Trio: Ahhh! *(sung)* Heavenly House Coffee—The Biblical Blend!

Flute: Taste and see that the Lord is good!

(MANNA MIX theme)

Trimbal: Now, that sounds like an invitation to the bakery shop at the Manna Mix Baking Company! The perfect complement to a BIG cup of Heavenly House Coffee!

Trio: *(sung)* Taste and see that the Lord is good.
Taste and see that the Lord is good.
Taste and see that the Lord is good.
Mmmm Mmmm. The Lord is good!

Cymbal: Manna Mix! Ready-made goodness in every bite! Variety and flavor for that healthy way to start your day!

Flute: Taste and see that the Lord is good!

Trio: *(sung)* Mmmm Mmmm. The Lord is good!

Announcer: That's Heavenly House Coffee and Manna Mix—as close as the Bible nearest YOU!

(TOYTOWN theme up—Larry, Moe, & Charlie step to microphones in silly hats)

Larry: Is it a broom?

Moe: Is it a mop?

Charlie: No, it's—

All: MARSHALL MISSION ACTION FIGURES!

Charlie: That's right, folks! Marshall Mission, Janitor Man—defender of all that is clean and pure—he who cleans whiter than snow—Marshall Mission and his faithful assistant, Brillo Boy, are at a Toytown near YOU!

Larry: Wow! A whole arsenal of cleaning supplies to sponge away even the toughest dirt!

Moe: Look! Here's the Scrubbing Bubbles Super Soaker! Set it on super-suds and stun your friends with its cleaning power!

Larry: My little brother loves his Marshall Mission Sponge-o-Matic capsules for bath time fun!

Charlie: And now, at a Toytown near YOU—the new Marshall Mission Fortress Buster! A special mixture of soap-on-a-rope suds that dissolves the sticky build-up of the fiercest fortress of muck and grime!

Larry: Yahooooo! Marshall Mission Secret Soap-on-a Rope sending scum and villainy straight to the sewer!

Moe: It's clean-free fun for a life-time!

Charlie: And all Marshall Mission products are guaranteed throughout eternity!

Larry: Plus—while supplies last . . .

All: The Frenzy Fortress!!

Charlie: Yes, folks! It's that nasty Fortress of Frenzy, as featured in the popular radio action drama, "The Adventures of Marshall Mission: Christmas Takes a Holiday!" The Fortress of Frenzy, built-up and cemented together with the deceptive lies of Hustle and Bustle's filth and foulness. Now, you at home can make the walls of that fortress come a' tumblin' down using your own supplies of Marshall Mission and Brillo Boy Action Figures, soap suds, cleansers and mops!

Larry: Like Joshua in the battle of Jericho, just swing your rope and throw your soap!

All: And those walls come a' tumblin' down!

Charlie: No more filthy rags or frenzy here! And all it takes is a trip to—

All: TOYTOWN!

Charlie: Visit a Toytown nearest you, today!

(TOYTOWN music ends)

(MARSHALL MISSION theme up)

Announcer: And now the conclusion of, "The Adventures of Marshall Mission: Christmas Takes a Holiday." When we last left our heroes, Marshall Mission and Brillo Boy had jumped aboard the Frenzy Express choo-chooing its way through a dark and sooty train tunnel to the very threshold of His Most High Grinchness and the Frenzy Fortress where poor Miss Frieda—all caught up in the Hustle and Bustle of the holiday season—had been carried away, running aimlessly in circles; busy doing this, believing that, and buying those—living on a treadmill of confusion and exhaustion. To be sure, Christmas had taken a holiday from her heart and mind. The emptiness of Frenzy, wrapped in Fear, brings no Truth or Joy at all. It's up to our own Marshall Mission, Janitor Man, to clean up this frenzied mess. Can he restore clear vision and focus to this merry season.

(Fade MARSHALL MISSION THEME; Loud sound effects of train whistle and train engine)

Brillo Boy: Eureka Vacuums, Marshall Mission! The train is finally slowing down!

Marshall: We must have arrived! I can tell by all the gaudy glitter and tentacles of tinsel! Shield your eyes, Brillo Boy! This is no heavenly glow we have happened upon! There! There's a nice soft spot to land in! That sandy patch up ahead!

Brillo Boy: Can't we just climb down when the train stops? It would be neater. My steel wool hair is already so wiry and windblown from hanging off the side of the smoke-stack all the way!

Marshall: We can't take the chance of being seen! We must preserve the element of surprise! I have a conditioning rinse in my utility belt that will whip your steel ends back into shape in a snap—with no rusty side-effects!

(Sound effect of landing after a fall; grunting as they land; train engine and whistle fade)

Brillo Boy: Eeewww! What kind of sand is this, Marshall Mission? It's all gritty and sticky!

Marshall: Brillo Boy, didn't you put on your protective shield before we left this morning? That sand should be rolling right off your stainless steel skin!

Brillo Boy: I'm sorry, Marshall Mission, I forgot. I was so distracted by my Christmas cookies baked with Manna Mix flour, powders, and spices, that I plumb forgot to finish my armor plating for the day!

Marshall: Let this be a lesson to you! Don't start your day without your full armor! Here now, stand still and I'll sweep you clean!

(Sound effect of broom and spray)

Brillo Boy: Mmmmm! Clean and shiny and armor-all ready! I'll never leave home without my shielding again!

Marshall Mission: Certainly! You must be able to outshine the counterfeit glimmer of all this gaudy glow surrounding us! Ugh! The world and its ways—shield your eyes, my boy! You and I know that there is only one true Light at Christmas. Perhaps, if we had been shining brighter from across the hall, Miss Frieda might not have been led astray to place her trust, time, and energy into such a fruitless holiday frenzy.

Frieda: Busy! Busy! Busy! Busy!

Marshall: Exactly. Too much busyness will choke the "merry" out of any "Christmas."

Frieda: Busy! Busy! Busy! Busy!

Marshall: Point taken, Brillo Boy. You don't have to repeat yourself.

Brillo Boy: But, Marshall Mission! I didn't say anything!

Marshall: I distinctly heard you say . . .

Frieda: Busy! Busy! Busy! Busy!

Marshall: There! You're doing it again!

Brillo Boy: But, it wasn't me!

Frieda: Busy! Busy! Busy!

Marshall: Not you!

Frieda: Busy! Busy! Busy!

Brillo Boy: Could it be . . .

Frieda: Busy! Busy! Busy!

Marshall Mission & Brillo Boy: MISS FRIEDA!

Marshall: There! Through those trees! The ones dripping with tinsel and balls and every tasteless trimming to be found at your local Dollar Store!

Brillo Boy: I see, Marshall Mission!

Marshall & Brillo Boy: The Frenzy Fortress!!!

Frieda: Busy! Busy! Busy! Can't stop to talk now! Too much to do! Too much to do! Oh! I'll never get it done. I am absolutely exhausted! When will it end! When will it end! Trial! Trial! Turmoil and Trial!

Marshall: Ah-HA! It may be worse than I thought! She may not be simply wallowing in the Dungeon of Despair feeding on Fear and Anxiety. Miss Frieda could very well be running ragged on a holiday treadmill behind those frenzied fortressed walls, like a mouse spinning wheels in a cage. Miss Frieda! Can you hear me? It is I, Marshall Mission!

Brillo Boy: And that nice Brillo Boy from across the hall!

Marshall: We are here to rescue you!

Frieda: Busy! Busy! Busy! No time to be rescued! But, such a kind thought! I must buy something extra special for your Christmas stocking! Oh! Just another thing to do, do, do!

Marshall: Miss Frieda! There, Brillo Boy! Do you see—up there—as I surmised! The Frenzy Fortress!

(OMINOUS CHORD)

Marshall: I caught a glimpse of her on the Treadmill of Trials—through the window—at the top of the Tower of Turmoil.

Brillo Boy: How terrible!

Marshall: *(calling out)* Miss Frieda! Move to the window and we'll contrive a plan to help you escape!

Frieda: What? I'd have to dismantle all my delightful window decorations! Oh! He wouldn't like that! He wouldn't like that one bit!

Marshall: Wouldn't like it? Who wouldn't like it?

Frenzy: I WOULDN'T LIKE IT! NOT ONE BIT!

Brillo Boy: Marshall Mission! It's . . . it's . . .

Marshall: I see who it is! Ebenezer Frenzy! So! You believe you have our Miss Frieda caught up in your frenzy, do you?!

Frenzy: To be specific, she got caught up in Hustle and Bustle and carried away in my frenzy by her own choice!

Hustle & Bustle: *(mad laughter)* Shall we spin her up even more? Huh! Huh! Can we???

Marshall: Hustle and Bustle! I expected to meet up with YOU again! I recognized your foul stench the moment I jumped off the train!

Hustle & Bustle: Ooooo!

Hustle: Did you hear that, deary? Foul stench! Foul stench!

Bustle: Oooo! How rotten of him to say so!

Marshall: You corrupt vermin!

Hustle & Bustle: Oooo!

Hustle: I've never been so insulted in all my life!

Bustle: Oh! Frenzy! Can we keep him?! Huh? Can we?

Hustle: He really knows how to charm the chaos outta ya!

Frenzy: Now, now, my directionless darlings . . . Marshall Mission is too clean and orderly to live here.

Bustle: We can dirty him up a bit . . . and keep him distracted . . .

Hustle: How about we get him connected on a slew of social media accounts! With such an endless newsfeed of perversity and peril, he'll end up just as cluttered and confused as us!!

Marshall: Never! I just say no to newsfeeds! Prepare to be deactivated. Your Frenzy Fortress is coming down!

Frenzy: Not so fast! Miss Frieda stepped into the Hustle and Bustle of the holiday season of her own free will. She made the choice to spend her holiday in a Frenzy with no purpose or priorities. There's nothing you can do about it! *(evil laugh)*

Brillo Boy: That's right, Marshall Mission. If Miss Frieda wants to spend the holiday in a Frenzy . . .

Marshall: Tish-tosh! Miss Frieda has made the same mistake many people do. They FALL INTO a Frenzy when they believe a lie. They listen to too many voices and get trapped in unrealistic expectations. Only one thing can set her free!

Hustle & Bustle: *(laughing)* One thing? What's that?

Marshall Mission: The Truth!

Hustle & Bustle: The truth???

Marshall Mission: Only Truth sets captives free! Miss Frieda! Can you hear me?

Frenzy: No—she can't!

Miss Frieda: Yes, I can hear you!

Marshall Mission: It is I, Marshall Mission!

Miss Frieda: *(weak voice)* Hello?

Hustle: *(mimicking)* It is I, on a mission to Marshalls with 30% off all ladies' wear and men's pajamas now through midnight tonight! So hurry!

Brillo Boy: And me, that nice Brillo Boy from across the hall!

Miss Frieda: Across the hall?

Bustle: Across the hall and down the elevator to the second floor toy department where you'll find all your Barbie Dream House and Vacation Lodge accessories on sale at 25% off but only until midnight tonight! Hurry! Hurry! You can't miss this sale!

Miss Frieda: Busy! Busy!

Marshall Mission: Don't pay any attention to those other voices . . .

Frenzy: Don't pay any attention to THOSE other voices . . .

Hustle: You're late for the Soccer Team's Christmas Party!

Bustle: You were supposed to pick up the pizza . . .

Miss Frieda: Pizza . . . Barbie . . . soccer? Busy! Busy!

Marshall Mission: Miss Frieda! They're only trying to confuse you. You're not on a soccer team!

Brillo Boy: You don't even have any kids who could be on a soccer team!

Frenzy: Did you get all your Christmas cards done yet??? All that gift wrapping?

Miss Frieda: Christmas cards?

Frenzy: You MUST mail everything by the 15th or it may not get there!

Miss Frieda: Oh! Post office, then pizza . . .

Marshall Mission: No! Frenzy!

Miss Frieda: Busy! Busy! Busy! Ugggghhhh!

Brillo Boy: *(increase volume)* **And it came to pass in those days . . .**

(Sound Engineer begins to build block wall)

Frenzy: *(sudden panic)* What was that?

Marshall Mission: Brilliant, Brillo Boy! **. . . a decree went out from Caesar Augustus that all the world should be taxed . . .**

Miss Frieda: Taxed? I must pay more tax? Too busy . . . too busy . . . too taxing!

Brillo Boy: **So all went to be registered, everyone to his own city.**

Hustle: So go! Go! GO!

Bustle: Go-Go! GO-GO!

Miss Frieda: Go! Go? Where?

Marshall Mission: **And Joseph also went up from Galilee, out of the city of Nazareth, into Judea, to the city of David, which is called Bethlehem.**

Brillo Boy: **. . . to be registered with Mary, his betrothed wife, who was with child.**

Frenzy: FOUL! Marshall Mission! You're playing dirty now! No more! No more!

Miss Frieda: More? More? Yes . . . more . . .

Frenzy: NO more!

Hustle & Bustle: NO MORE!

Brillo Boy: **So it was, that while they were there, the days were completed for her to be delivered.**

Marshall Mission: **And she brought forth her firstborn Son, and wrapped Him in swaddling cloths, and laid Him in a manger . . .**

Brillo Boy: **. . . because there was no room for them in the inn.**

Frenzy: No!! Not the manger!!

Marshall Mission: **Now there were in the same country shepherds living out in the fields, keeping watch over their flock by night.**

Hustle: Shepherds! Not the shepherds!!

Brillo Boy: **And behold, an angel of the Lord stood before them . . .**

Bustle: Angels?!

Frenzy, Hustle & Bustle: NO ANGELS!!!

Marshall Mission: **. . . and the glory of the Lord shone round about them, and they were greatly afraid.**

Frenzy, Hustle & Bustle: No! No! Stop! No more!

Miss Frieda: More? Please, more?

(THE FIRST NOEL instrumental music up in background)

Brillo Boy: **Then the angel said unto them, "Do not be afraid, for behold, I bring you good tidings of great joy which will be to all people. For unto you is born this day in the city of David, a Savior, who is Christ the Lord."**

Marshall Mission: **And suddenly there was with the angel a multitude of the heavenly host praising God and saying: "Glory to God in the highest,**

and on earth PEACE, good will toward men!"

Miss Frieda: PEACE! Peace! I want . . .

Frenzy, Hustle & Bustle: NO! Wait! Stop!

Miss Frieda: I want . . . **PEACE!**

(THE FIRST NOEL music stops abruptly)

Marshall Mission: Now, Brillo Boy! Soap-on-a-Rope Factor "Peace Be Still 100%!"

Brillo Boy: Here, Marshall Mission!

Marshall & Brillo: SOAP-ON-A-ROPE AWAY!!

(Soap hits block wall tower which comes tumbling down)

(Music triumph FANFARE chords)

Miss Frieda: I'm free! I'm free!

Marshall Mission: Miss Frieda, how nice to see you again. Are you enjoying a PEACEFUL Christmas season?

Frenzy: FOUL! Look what you did to my Frenzy Fortress!! Rubble! Stones and rubble!

Marshall Mission: Your Frenzy Fortress was just a filthy smoke-screen blocking the true Reason for the Season with all your vile distractions.

Miss Frieda: But, I really thought I was doing all I should to properly prepare for the holidays.

Marshall Mission: You mean, HOLY days, Miss Frieda. How did getting caught up in Hustle and Bustle, and being carried away in a Frenzy, help you celebrate the joy filled birth of our Savoir, Jesus Christ?

Hustle & Bustle: *(in pain)* Oooooo! What he just said! Uggghhh!!

Frenzy: Oh! The effrontery! I am undone!!!

Miss Frieda: Well, sometimes I feel so lost and lonely in this scary, wide, old world. I guess I thought, if I just stayed busy enough, surrounding myself with the trappings and distractions of the season . . . then maybe I wouldn't be so lonely . . . and lost.

Brillo Boy: And, did that work?

Miss Frieda: No. Before I knew it, I was locked in a prison of doing this, and that, running here and there, and I forgot about making time to just . . . be . . .

Marshall Mission: What is it you want to BE, Miss Frieda?

Miss Frieda: I want to be . . . STILL. At PEACE. Deep in my heart. With JOY.

Frenzy, Hustle & Bustle: *(in pain)* Aaarrruuughh!

Marshall Mission: What else have you learned, Miss Frieda?

Miss Frieda: Well, I know now that Mr. Frenzy here, with all the promises of his gaudy glimmerings, is just a big fat liar. He is nothing compared to the golden glow of the Truth of Christmas. And, if I ever go looking for my heart's desire again, I won't look any farther than God, Himself—who loved me so much that He sent His only Son—that baby in the manger—and if I believe in Him, His life, and death, and resurrection—then I'll truly be . . . not lost—but found; not lonely—but alive and living in the TRUE Christmas Spirit—new life in Jesus Christ.

Frenzy, Hustle & Bustle: *(painful moans)* Arrrrruuuuuggggghh! That name!!!!

Miss Frieda: That NAME is what celebrating Christmas should be all about. Smh!

Frenzy: *(angry)* UGH! Come on, Hustle and Bustle. We're useless here now. She's thinking for herself. We'll go build another fortress in somebody else's heart and mind. There's always another . . . *(evil laugh)*

Marshall Mission: FRENZY! *(evil laugh cuts off)* We SHALL meet again!

Brillo Boy: Yeah! And, when we do, we'll be sure to bust your dust!

(Dust Buster revs up)

Frenzy, Hustle and Bustle: *(in fear)* Aaarrrrraugh!! Frenzy! Frenzy! Retreat!!! Run Away!!!! *(FANFARE music up)*

Marshall Mission: Come, Miss Frieda, let us return to our homes and Brillo Boy and I will have your apartment Spic-n-Span in no time, aglow in the true Christmas Spirit of peace on earth, good will toward men.

(Music up for HARK THE HERALD ANGELS SING)

Announcer: And so ends Marshall Mission's Christmas Adventure. Marshall Mission, Brillo Boy and Miss Frieda enjoyed a quiet Christmas together pondering these things in their hearts with pizza, Pepsi, and freshly baked Christmas cookies made with the flours, powders, and spices from the Manna Mix Baking Company.

Marshall: Don't forget that delicious after dinner cup of Heavenly House Coffee – the Biblical Blend!

All: Taste and see that the Lord IS good!

Announcer: As we bid a fond farewell to our heroes who saved the Christmas holy day in Miss Frieda's heart and mind, we hope that the true meaning of Christmas be saved in your heart and mind, overflowing with peace and joy and God's richest blessings!

(HARK THE HERALD ANGELS SING fade; WEATHER music up)

Announcer: And now, a final holiday weather word from our own Wilhelmina Weather. What kind of broadcasting weather can we expect, Wilhelmina?

(Wilhelmina puts on halo and angel wings)

Wilhelmina: This just in from a Christmas Angel! As far as my holiday weather reports are concerned, you may have noticed a bit of confusion on a global scale. There is no indication that the forecast will change. In fact—it may get worse. Even so, we can still expect to broadcast in every sort of weather this Christmas season. Neither rain, nor hail, nor sleet, nor snow, can keep God's love and the Reason for the Season from its appointed rounds. Who shall separate us from the love of Christmas?

Shall trouble and tornados, or hardship and hurricanes, or persecution and precipitation, or famine and fog, or danger and dry spells, or sword and storms? No, in all these things we are more than conquerors through God who loves us. Let the Son-Light shine in the darkness—Peace on Earth, good will to all men! Like I always say, no matter the weather, it's always a good WPWP day!

All: Wow! That is GOOD NEWS!

(MANNA MIX THEME)

Announcer: We'd like to thank our sponsors, Marshall Mission Action Figures at a Toytown near you, Heavenly House Coffee, the Biblical Blend, and the Manna Mix Baking Company . . .

Trio: Taste and see that the Lord is good.
Taste and see that the Lord is good.
Taste and see that the Lord is good.
Manna Mix, for all your baking needs!
Mmmm, the Lord is good.

Dawson: But for now, on behalf of Marshall Mission . . .

Sean: Brillo Boy . . .

Jack: Ebenezer Frenzy . . .

Cassidy: Wilhelmina Weather . . .

Hope, Jordan & Larissa: And the entire staff here at WPWP Radio . . .

Wiley: We wish you all a very Merry Christmas and a happy New Year!!

All: A poem, a song, some laughter to go along
With our joyful wish this season,
That you remember Christ, the reason
We celebrate Christmas . . .

(Music up full for HARK THE HERALD ANGELS SING or another Christmas carol of your choice. Entire cast sings. Invite audience to sing-a-long)

PRODUCTION NOTES & STUDY GUIDE

Page 43 ~ Set & Props Checklist
Suggestions for props and silly hats. Some of the props/hats are required, some may be customized for your group and availability. They will be noted as such on the checklist.

Page 45 ~ Music
Tunes are designed for an electronic keyboard with student performers. Sheet music for the original tunes are included plus itemized direction for acquiring the music for other tunes mentioned in the script.

Page 51 ~ Costumes
Keeping things vintage/retro—suggestions are made for recreating mid-20th century fashions and hats.

Page 55 ~ Miscellaneous Helps
Tips for memorizing lines, ministering to your cast as a director in a discipleship focused style, and more.

Page 58 ~ Vocabulary Enrichment
Necessary for all student casts as some of the vocabulary and pronunciation may be challenging.

Page 59 ~ Bible Study
Scriptures and biblical principles touched upon within the context of the story are noted for research and discussion.

Page 62 ~ History of Radio Academic Assignments
Use the prologue lines to teach the history of radio via student research, essay, display projects, and discussion.

Set Checklist

Most of the set pieces are common items found in a school or church. You can keep things as no frills or as fanciful as you like. I am listing the basics here. If you have a set designer available to you, research interior images of mid-20th century radio stations and plan your set with art deco artistic touches for a more vintage feel. Refer to the set notes in the script for stage layout. You will need for a bare bones set:

[ ] 8 foot table covered with black cloth
[ ] 6 foot table covered with black cloth
[ ] 7 chairs
[ ] 2 stools
[ ] 2 standing microphones
[ ] 2 black music stands
[ ] 2 black binders with full scripts (on music stands)
[ ] Electronic keyboard (plugged in)
[ ] 2 each 4-6 foot pre-lit Christmas trees

Note: When I produced this play, I had access to a full size vintage wooden radio which I placed center stage between the three chairs on stage left and stage right. The top of the radio was level with the 8 foot table on an upper platform so the Sound Engineer and Wilhelmina working the sound effects and keyboard weren't blocked.

Refer to this vintage table radio illustration (left) and the microphone illustration on the title page for period visuals. You can enlarge them and create full size faux set pieces.

Expand Your Set Design: Research online to see photos of what the interior of 1930-1940 radio stations looked like and create set pieces to evoke that time period. Anything Art Deco will do the trick. If you have the budget and art skills available to you to create a more complex set, then make it happen. This is a great opportunity to provide unity study academics in art history, social/cultural history, and teamwork.

Prop Checklist

[ ] 2 boxes of Christmas tree decorations
[ ] Santa hat
[ ] Reindeer antlers hat
[ ] Large APPLAUSE sign
[ ] Large ON THE AIR sign
[ ] 2 coconut halves for varied sounds
[ ] Teacup and saucer for clinking sound
[ ] Pitcher of water for pouring sound
[ ] Plate of cookies
[ ] Large fur hat
[ ] Marshall Mission hat
[ ] Brillo Boy hat
[ ] Dinner bell
[ ] Large clump of wrapping paper for rustling sounds
[ ] Dust Buster plugged in
[ ] Something to make "banging" sound
[ ] Something to make "door creaking" sound
[ ] Larry, Moe, Charlie silly hats
[ ] Large sun hat and oversized sunglasses
[ ] Umbrella hat or umbrella
[ ] Wooden train whistle
[ ] Two large Good & Plenty candy boxes to shake for train engine sound
[ ] Doorbell ring sound
[ ] Hand broom and spray bottle sound
[ ] 12 large wooden blocks to build fortress wall
[ ] Soap-on-a-rope
[ ] Angel halo and wings

Music

In the original tunes for *Christmas Takes a Holiday*, only the melody lines and guitar chords are provided here. The music is noted in the script as particular "themes" and can be performed as simple or as complex as your group's musicians can muster. Many young people are very talented musicians and can embellish the melody lines with chords or other instruments such as bass, drums, flute, violin, or trumpet. If you can't have an orchestra, one or two students schooled in plucking out the single notes on cue on an electronic keyboard is sufficient. Here are a few specific suggestions in managing the musical elements of this play:

Built-in Tunes: Make use of appropriate built-in tunes in the electronic keyboard where you'll find pre-recorded beats and short snippets of tunes that can be used for the opening WPWP music theme and the fanfares. This requires only the touch of a button for the Sound Engineer if your cast has limited musical gifts.

Bare Bones Basics: I originally produced this play with a wide age range of elementary level homeschool students. None of them had begun music lessons to where they could handle anything beyond plunking out the melody line on the keyboard. The gal playing Wilhelmina, who also provided assistant Sound Engineer duties, worked with a music mentor to perfect the simple tunes for the commercial jingles and story themes. A karaoke soundtrack of *Deck the Halls* opened the show. Pre-recorded keyboard tunes filled in as noted above. Sheet music to traditional Christmas carols are not included here.

Take It Up a Notch: Older students will be able to master the comedic timing and delivery of the lines with more confidence, and may have more musical skills to bring to the production table. Stretch your cast to contribute as they are able and find unique ways to use the talents of your group—especially in music.

Pre-Record a Custom Soundtrack: If you have the skills and equipment, you can pre-record a small band of your students or volunteer musicians (perhaps the church or school worship team) playing all the music and make your own soundtrack that is cued by the technical director running the microphones and lighting equipment. This frees your cast to the stage performance only.

On-Stage Live Band Music: With a small cast of only nine performers, you may have some students who are available to perform strictly as an onstage band. They can use the simple instruments or add others as noted above, accompanying all the action live just like the session band musicians in the studios of radio stations of the past.

Choreography: Even though this is radio, the show notes that they are aware of a live studio audience. Lucille Ball was a huge radio comedy show star prior to her *I Love Lucy* success on television. Radio studio audiences loved her body language and facial mugging in the delivery of her lines and roared with laughter, adding to the entertainment value of the radio show for listeners at home. Adding a few dance moves to the commercial jingles and coaching your actors to use all of their body with facial expressions in line delivery polishes the performance, adding energy to line delivery.

Tune List

Deck the Halls—Public domain. Use karaoke soundtrack or traditional sheet music from the Christmas carol songbook of your choice.

WPWP Theme—Use an upbeat pre-recorded tune from an electronic keyboard or a couple of measures from an upbeat tune of your choice.

Heavenly House Coffee Theme—As provided here. Music and lyrics © 2016 Pageant Wagon Publishing. See page 8.

Manna Mix Baking Company Theme—As provided here. Music and lyrics © 2016 Pageant Wagon Publishing. See page 8.

Weather Theme—Plunk out any treble note in a faux morse code staccato—four counts of four.

Secret Agent Theme—Plunk out a staccato beat reminiscent of the old *Batman* T.V. show theme—three counts of eight; "Na-na na-na na-na na-na Na-Naaaa." Do you work with musicians who can come up with a better few beats for this theme? Go with it!

Marshall Mission Theme—As provided here. Music and lyrics © 2016 Pageant Wagon Publishing. See page 9.

O Little Town of Bethlehem—Public domain. Use karaoke soundtrack or traditional sheet music from the Christmas carol songbook of your choice.

Jingle Bells Broken Record—Plunk out the first ten notes of Jingle Bells from any traditional sheet music of Christmas songs over and over and over and over and over again.

Fanfare—See if there is something that works in the pre-recorded tunes of an electronic keyboard. Experiment with different instruments. Google "fanfare tunes" and listen online to samples of tunes you may want to use. Consult with a musician friend to settle on a choice. All you need is a simple four count tune.

The First Noel—Public domain. Use karaoke soundtrack or traditional sheet music from the Christmas carol songbook of your choice.

Hark the Herald Angels Sing—Public domain. Use karaoke soundtrack or traditional sheet music from the Christmas carol songbook of your choice.

Heavenly House Coffee

Arranged by Andrew Finn

Manna Mix Baking Company Tune

Arranged by Andrew Finn

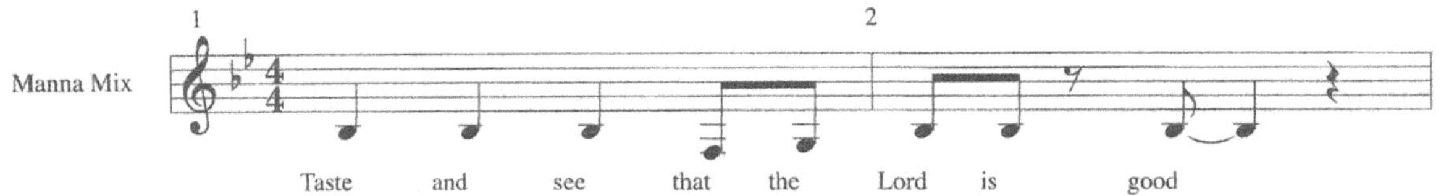

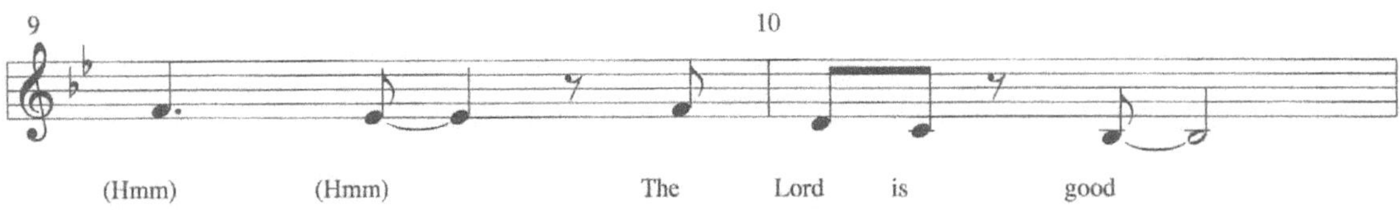

Marshall Mission Theme

Arranged by Andrew Finn

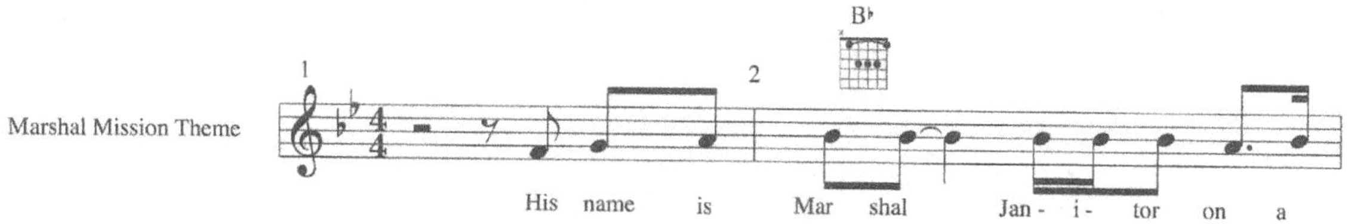
Marshal Mission Theme
1
2
B♭
His name is Mar shal Jan - i - tor on a

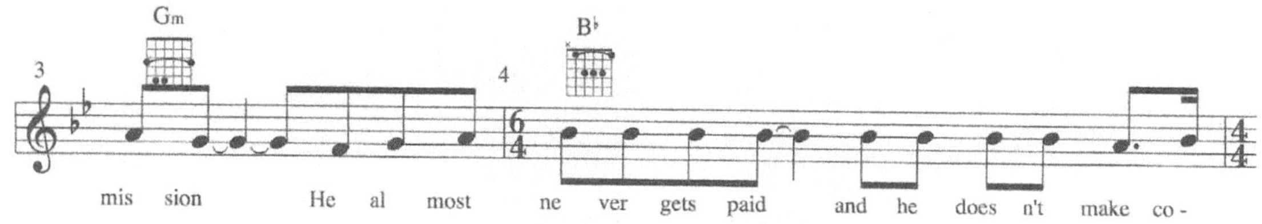
3
Gm
4
B♭
mis sion He al most ne ver gets paid and he does n't make co -

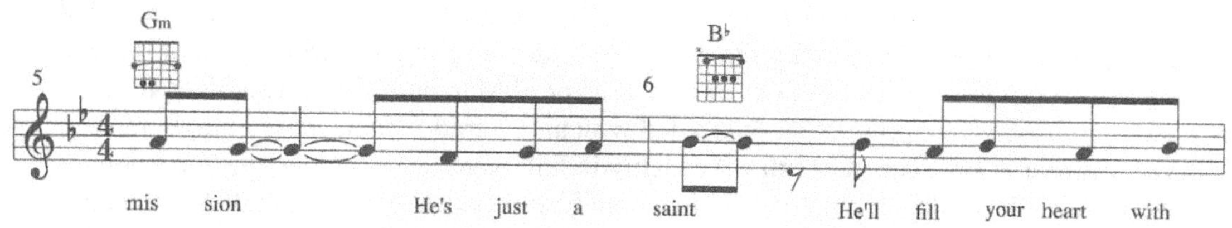
5
Gm
6
B♭
mis sion He's just a saint He'll fill your heart with

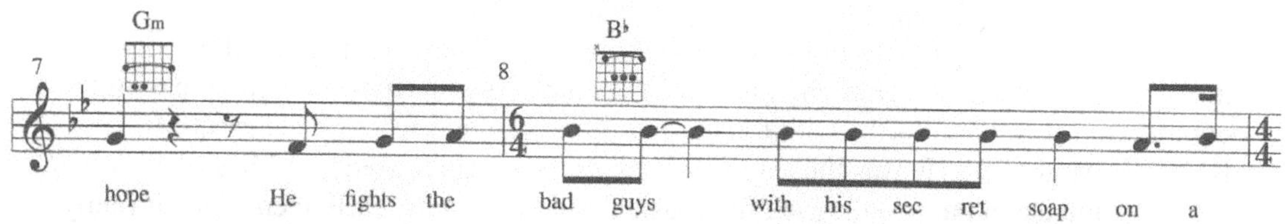
7
Gm
8
B♭
hope He fights the bad guys with his sec ret soap on a

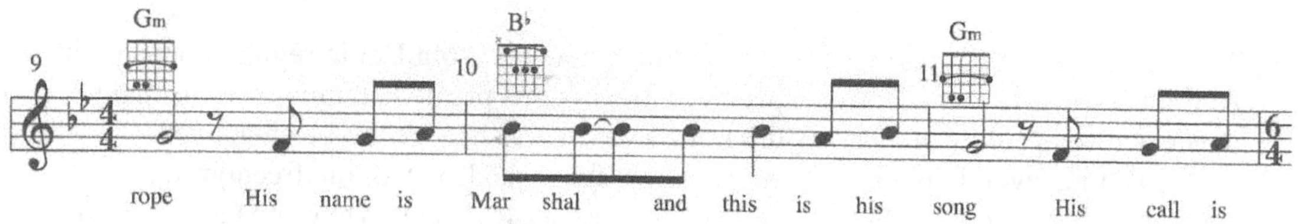
9
Gm
10
B♭
11
Gm
rope His name is Mar shal and this is his song His call is

B♭
Gm
B♭
Gm
B♭
Gm
clear he rids the world of dirt and of wrong
Mar shal Mar shal
Mis sion
Mar shal Mar shal
Mis sion

A Note of Thanks

The Adventures of Marshall Mission: Christmas Takes a Holiday, is the second Marshall Mission adventure I wrote and produced. It was adapted from an earlier work of mine for a homeschool theatre class in 2009. The character of Marshall Mission and idea for a radio drama onstage production originated with an 8th grade drama class I taught ten years earlier at East Gate Christian Academy in Fall River, Massachusetts. The students were a big part of developing the campy comedy and character of Marshall Mission, as well as writing the music for the play. I worked with some strong musicians, then in the early stages of their career.

Special thanks to Andrew Finn for revisiting those days with me in taking the scribbled notes from the time and arranging them with the use of some techno-magic in one of the computer programs he works with today as youth pastor and worship leader at Master Builder's Ministries. He was the lead musician in the original Marshall Mission in *WWJD Wireless* and had a hand in drafting the music at the time in his early teens. He currently teaches on staff in the same school where he was once the student and I was the teacher. Teaching and learning come full circle!

To be sure, I'm still in touch with many former students—but I'm in regular contact with Andrew as he is my son. I'm very proud of him and his precious family, and his many musical accomplishments serving the Lord today. I was honored to be an active participant in developing his gifts, and so thankful to the Lord for the freedom we enjoyed in our years of both Christian and homeschool settings to explore God's Word and all things academically and creatively and in Christ.

Kathryn Ross
July 2016

Costumes

Costume decisions may vary depending on the age of your cast. Thrift stores are the best place to find the basics for costuming this show. However, if you are working with young children, you may need to do some alterations on larger sized clothing to balance the look and fit. You're going for an adult look on a child's frame. Children's sizes in the styles you'd need are not readily available—even though you can keep it very simple with a uniform look in both boys and girls. Here are some suggestions for evoking a 1930's-1940's look:

Bare Bones Basics: Keep it simple.

FOR GIRLS—a plain white blouse buttoned up to the neck, full black skirt at knee length or just below the knee (no mini-skirts), white or nude hose and black flats. Top it off with a Period Hat (see below) to give this plain Jane look a vintage flair.

FOR BOYS—white long sleeve button-down shirt with large bow ties, suspenders, black pants, black socks, black dress shoes. Top it off with a Period Hat (see below) to give this look a vintage flair.

Take It Up a Notch: Spend some time reading the excellent articles on fashions for men and women in the 1930's and 1940's via the excellent historic attire website at **Vintage Dancer**, http://vintagedancer.com/. Just click on the tab for your decade of choice, 1900 through the 1960's. If your cast is older, kick your costuming into high gear with trips to thrift shops where you may find old styles to mimic the 1940's. For instance:

FOR LADIES, you'll notice from the photos of some of the dresses popular in the 1940's, that dresses from the 1980's used similar styling, most notably the large shoulder pads. You may find fitted blazers with shoulder pads and knee length A-line skirts or full swing skirts, or dresses with shoulder pads, high waist, and full skirts that copy the 1940's look.

FOR MEN, clothing should include the basics as noted above, but you may want to add a V-neck vest sweater, and be sure pants fit AT THE WAIST—not hanging low on the hips as is currently in vogue. On the Vintage Dancer website there are lots of images from the era to help you—plus patterns available to make authentic styles from scratch. Also, watching a few MGM movie musicals from the era will give you a host of ideas for fashion in vibrant VistaVision and Cinemascope Technicolor.

Silly Prop Hats: Score the goal for the Sound Engineers to make their sound effect activity more interesting with a collection of silly hats. For instance, in the Prop List you'll note there is mention of a train engineer hat and a train conductor's hat. Both of these costume hats are available at any costume or party shop—a virtual playground of hats can be found there. During the train scene, the Sound Engineer can wear the train engineer hat while blowing the train whistle and waving the flashlight, while Wilhelmina wears the train conductor hat and shakes the Good & Plenty candy boxes to mimic the sound of the choo-choo. What other Silly Prop Hats can you make a part of the Sound Engineer shtick?

Period Hat Tricks: Score the goal of a period look with vintage hats. Fedoras for men and a host of vintage styles for women. Consult the online resources at **Vintage Dancer** http://vintagedancer.com/ where you'll find a host of articles, photographs, and more for historical attire, make-up tips, and Period Hat visuals under the tab for your decade of choice, 1900 through 1960's. Comb thrift stores and antique shops for the goods.

Character Hat Tricks: Score the goal for distinguishing your character roles with special hats changed out by the actors when they are playing their parts in the Marshall Mission episode segments. Each actor keeps their Character Hats tucked under their chair for easy access, changing in and out of it as the story progresses. Wear the Period Hats for the in-between commercials and weather reports and the Character Hats for the storyline. Note the photos on the following page showing the original young cast in their simple Character Hats.

Marshall Mission Hat (left)—What kind of hat do you think Marshall Mission would wear? Keeping it simple and budget friendly, I purchased a yellow foamy construction worker kid's hat (from an arts and crafts store like Michaels), kitchen sponges, scrub brush, and a large letter "M"—and with a bit of glue-gun magic, Marshall Mission had a hat.

Brillo Boy (right)—The script is pretty clear as to what Brillo Boy looks like. His name alone provides direction for creating a headpiece for a character described as having a head full of steel wool ends. So, to that end, I purchased another foamy black hat from Michaels and cut off the rim. I also got a large bag of steel wool from the hardware store. Spread out the steel wool and glue it liberally on the black hat base for a perfect Brillo Boy look.

Hustle, Bustle and Frenzy: These characters are gaudy Christmas personified. I found some sparkle, metallic chain links for tree trimming in vibrant colors. The lights on the stage picked up the sparkles in the chains and make them sizzle. All I did was glue them onto plastic headbands. They bounced around and were easy to put on and off between scene changes. To distinguish Frenzy, a red devil mask and horns did the trick and is available at any costume shop such as Party City.

Silly Hats: As mentioned above in the comments, a host of silly hats for the sound effects and props station adds to the entertainment value of the scenes. Other Silly Hats featured might be jester hats for the Larry, Moe, and Charlie characters.

As you work through production, use your imagination and the imagination of your cast to find ways to interpret some of the storytelling elements with sight gags. But, sprinkle them wisely so as not to detract from the storytelling. Too much salt makes you spit out the food, leaving you thirsty.

Miscellaneous Helps

Memorization: When your cast struggles with memorizing lines by the due date—lend them a hand with these tips—make it fun and it will be memorable!

1. Read the passage carefully and decide what it means. When you know the meaning of a passage and how it relates to the story, it is easier to memorize.

2. Break the passage into shorter phrases that seem to go together with common thoughts or words.

3. Memorize the easy lines first—then add the longer, harder ones.

4. Create a "daisy-chain." Learn one section of a line. Memorize a second and add that onto the first. Add the third part and the fourth in the same manner, and so on.

5. Work on longer segments over a period of days, mastering each segment in smaller bits.

6. Find the rhythm of the passage and memorize it with a beat like a nursery rhyme or poem. Shakespeare is perfect for this type of musical memorization.

7. Choose a keyword for each phrase and use it as an anchor in case you draw a blank.

8. Set the words to a familiar tune or make up one of your own.

9. Look for mnemonic devices like the repetition of certain sounds, how a list of key words might lend itself to an acronym, or the way some words might appear in alphabetical order.

Cast Ministry: Whether you're directing in a church, school or community theatre venue, your priority should be ministry to your cast first. Incorporate these habits into your directing style . . .

1. Hold your cast to a high standard of production, requiring them to put forth continued effort in perfecting their roles. Their hard work prepares them for future challenges, and the rewards of their work will be their joy come opening night.

2. Require promptness at rehearsals and deadlines for line memorization. When everyone in the cast pulls their weight, as a team you'll be strong. Don't allow cast members to become a drain on the hard work of others because they show a lax approach to their part. Do all to the Glory of God.

3. Discern the actor in need of extra support to perfect their role. Make time to mentor them on the side to accommodate any unique learning styles.

4. Fully support your cast by thinking ahead to their needs in each rehearsal. Shepherd them through the process by clearly communicating your blocking instructions.

5. Act out challenging scenes or line delivery yourself. Break down stage movements, vocal beats/dramatic pauses, or facial expressions, into small parts. Personally demonstrate your vision and encourage your cast to imitate you. Show—don't just tell—when directing.

6. Listen to your actors. Allow them to be participants in interpreting their roles, taking ownership of the part they are playing. Good direction draws out an actor's inspired performance, balancing directorial vision with what they can bring to it.

7. Disciple your cast throughout the production period in all ways. The nurturing attention you give to them pays off in the end product—in both their hearts and resulting stage performances. Never drive a performance out of them—always lead, inspiring from the front.

8. Critique cast performances with constructive, encouraging words. Never criticize using negative or degrading language, humiliating cast members openly. Acting requires the freedom of uninhibited speaking

and movement. Coarse critiques may constrict your actors, producing the opposite effect than what your correction had hoped for. Always critique with creative instruction, not condemnation.

9. Notice the unique achievements and character traits in each of your cast members throughout production. Create an Award Certificate for each member. Present to each with affirming words at a follow-up event celebrating a job well done.

Ultimately, if you perform your director job in the spirit of a mentor/shepherd, nurturing your cast with a balance of firm production requirements and loving encouragement, the end product of your play will take care of itself with shouts of "Bravo!"

Campy Comedy: The board acting necessary for producing this play allows the cast to "ham" it up and have fun with performances just a bit over the top. The best example of this type of comedy acting is seen in the old ***Batman* television series** from the 1960's. View an episode with your students and discuss what you observed in the performances. How can you mimic some of that campy-comedy style into the Marshall Mission scenes, while delivering some of the more serious lines toward the end of the episode with sincerity and truth. Discuss which lines you'll give special attention to in this way. Help your cast hit the following marks in performance and you'll have a great show.

- **Vocal Variety** is imperative. Experiment with different vocal inflections in line delivery and characterization.
- **Expressive Body Language** keep energy flowing which helps in the delivery of lines and makes for greater visual interest.
- **Projection of Voice** is a must—even with microphones, strong projection of the voice is commanding and shows confidence,
- **Diction and Pronunciation** of words requires practice. Some of the words are a mouthful—especially when strung together in some of the wordy phrases.
- **Timing** is important. Don't rush through the lines. Take your time and pronounce each syllable and ending consonant.
- **Dramatic Pauses are** very effective. Use wisely and well.

Vocabulary

I originally produced this Christmas themed play with students as young as seven, having only recently learned to read. Some of the parts are very simple lines, easy to memorize and pronounce. Drawing a performance of the material out of young actors is usually the hardest part. Even though they tend to memorize quickly, many lack the life experience and confidence to deliver lines and develop characters that are three dimensional. Helping them keep their focus in a scene so they don't miss their cue is also another area where very young actors will struggle.

One thing I have learned—rehearsals will never give you a clear idea of what they will rise to on opening night with an audience. I am always pleasantly surprised!

I recommend this play is best performed by upper elementary and middle school or older students who may be more open to the broad acting necessary to make the show click. Even so, some of the words may not be familiar to all ages. I am including a few words you can review or add to spelling lists. These words also may pose a pronunciation challenge when spoken in the context of wordy lines. Use this list and add to it as necessary for your group.

Manna	Vicinity
Accumulation	Precipitation
Arsenal	Abode
Smattering	Delectable
Sumptuous	Pungent
Providential	Vulgar
Sufficient	Satisfying
Gaudy	Surmised
Vermin	Perversity

Recommended Dictionary for Word Study:
The Webster's 1828 Dictionary of the English Language is the best source for word definitions in keeping with a biblical worldview. Access it online at http://webstersdictionary1828.com/

Bible Study

This is the most important aspect in working with your cast— ministering God's Word to their hearts first, so that they fully understand what they are communicating in their performance. This is an excellent way to exercise skills in thinking and reasoning from a biblical worldview, with practical story application.

In this section I include Scripture references that inspire a line or principle within a particular scene. Have students look up the Scriptures and write them out. Discuss each in the early stages of production. Use the online Bible Gateway tool at https://www.biblegateway.com.

As you work through the scenes in smaller parts during blocking rehearsals, review the Scriptural principle behind the lines as part of the instruction. Lead discussion to guide critical thinking about how the Scripture or principle is illustrated in the story and how that same principle might be applied to their life. Comprehending the import of the lines go a long way towards those lines and scenes being played out with stronger delivery and understanding.

Heavenly House Coffee #1—pages 9-10
House of the Lord—Psalm 122:1
Sweet Smelling Aroma—Ephesians 5:2; Philippians 4:18
Goodness and mercy will follow—Psalm 23

Manna Mix Baking Company—page 10
Manna—Exodus 16:31-35
Taste and see—Psalm 34:8
Sweeten with honey—Psalm 119:103
Breads, muffins, pastries—Matthew 4:4; Luke 4:4

Marshall Mission Episode 1—pages 12-18
He's just a saint—Ephesians 2:18-20 Identity
He'll fill your heart with hope—Ephesians 3:8-9 Purpose
He fights the bad guys—2 Chronicles 7-8
His call is clear—2 Timothy 1:8-11
He rids the world of dirt and wrong—2 Corinthians 7:1; 1 John 1:9
Power to eliminate the stain of sin from the human heart—Luke 5: 24; Acts 26:18
Filthy rags to wash whiter than snow—Isaiah 64:6; Isaiah 1:18
Filth and Foul are afoot—1 Peter 5:8
Brave defender of greaseless countertops—Titus 1:9; Jude 3-4
Such a confused mess—1 Corinthians 14:33
Assault weapons of clutter, chaos, and confusion—James 3:16; 2 Timothy 3

Marshall Mission Episode 2—pages 22-25
Fear and Anxiety feeding her—1 John 4:18; Psalm 55:1-8
In the Dungeon of Despair—2 Corinthians 1:8
Never waver in our focus—Romans 4:20; Hebrews 10:23
Whisk away those tear stains—Isaiah 25:8
Set her clean free—Romans 6:16-23

Heavenly House Coffee #2—page 26
Heavenly House at my house—Joshua 24:15
The way to start your morning—Psalm 5:3; Psalm 59:16 Psalm 88:13
Nothing lukewarm here—Revelations 3:15-17
It's sufficient for me—2 Corinthians 12:9

Toytown—page 29
Walls come a tumblin' down—Hebrews 11:30

Marshall Mission Episode 3—pages 30-40
Don't start your day without your full armor—Ephesians 6:10-18
I am absolutely exhausted—Galatians 6:9
Treadmill of Trials/Tower of Turmoil—Job 30:17; Psalm 38:8; Contrast w/2 Corinthians 4:8-10
She made the choice—Proverbs 1:29
Yes, I can hear you—Romans 10:17
Fall into frenzy when they believe a lie—2 Timothy 3:13Psalm 73 Discuss principle connections
Only Truth sets captives free—John 8:32
And it came to pass in those days—Luke 2:1-14
Peace—Romans 14:17
Rubble! Stones and rubble—Joshua 6:20
Be still—Psalm 46; Psalm 46:10
I won't look any farther than God—Matthew 6:33
If I believe in Him—Acts 16:31; Romans 10:9
New life in Jesus Christ—Romans 6:4; 2 Corinthians 5:17
Retreat! Run away—James 4:7

Weather Report & Finale—pages 40-41
A bit of confusion on a global scale—2 Thess. 2; 2 Timothy 3; Romans 8:33-39
Celebrate Christmas—Psalm 33:1-5; 1 Peter 1:3; Ephesians 1:3; 2 Corinthians 1:3

Shepherd Your Cast & Crew

- *Make Christian discipleship a priority in your drama ministry.*
- *Use play producing as an opportunity to build relationships through shared experiences working in and living out God's Word.*
- *Shepherding your cast and crew, with a focus on pleasing God as an audience of One, invites the Holy Spirit to act as Executive Producer of your drama—ensuring God's best on opening night.*
- *Pray as a cast and crew for everyone who will see your drama—that God's will be done in their lives through the message of your drama.*
- *Give God the glory for the things He will do through your drama ministry!*

How did the advent of radio accomplish God's purposes in the cultural and world shaking events of the 20th century?

History of Radio Academic Assignments

In developing curriculum for a particular subject in Principle Approach Education®, I am first tasked with researching the history of a subject in relation to biblical truth and where the topic fits on an historical timeline. This is where I began my preparation—the history of radio.

From my study, I condensed the basic timeline facts into a series of lines relating the most important truths of the subject. These lines became the prologue for the production, providing backstory to both the cast and the audience. With the 8th grade students I taught, we spent more time on the academic particulars, culminating with listening and reviewing one of the most famous radio dramas ever broadcast.

The following is a reprint of the prologue broken into topic chunks. Begin your production time with a couple of weeks dedicated to this interesting study. Assign students topics to research and write about to expand their understanding. In so doing, you'll have opportunity for essays on radio inventor biographies, cultural changes due to radio, societal changes due to radio, impact of radio on world events, popular radio stars and programs, economic impact of commercial advertising using radio, and more.

If you homeschool, this study could become an entire semester unit study culminating in your homeschool co-op performing the play in the simplicity of a reader's theatre format for parents at home.

If you're using this in a Christian classroom, make the assignments worthy of extra credit or include it in language and history grades. For church groups, find ways to illustrate biblical principles into what you discover through your study—specifically how God providentially opens the doors to inventions at specific times in history to accomplish His purposes.

Early Stages of Development:

Almost two hundred years ago, **Michael Faraday** and **Joseph Henry** had an idea! They thought that an electrical current flowing in one wire could produce a current in a second wire, even if the two wires were not touching. They believed a wireless connection of electrical energy was possible. In the 1890's, **Guglielmo Marconi** sent the first wireless radio message across the English Channel. Soon, he had placed wireless radio sets in lighthouses all along the coast of England to send and receive Morse code during emergencies at sea.

The first wireless transmission of the human voice happened in 1906 when **Reginald Fessenden** spoke by radio from Brant Rock, Massachusetts, to ships in the Atlantic Ocean on Christmas Eve. Fessenden read from the Bible and a musician played a violin solo of sacred music. Afterward, listeners were invited to tune in next week at the same time for another broadcast program.

1. Assign students to write biographical sketches of Michael Faraday, Joseph Henry, Guglielmo Marconi, and Reginald Fessenden.
2. What character qualities did they exhibit to be able to achieve their scientific goals in the development of wireless radio?
3. The process of radio development did not happen overnight. What does this teach us about how God works out his plans and purposes for specific times in history? Plot radio development out on an historical timeline to better understand the cultural and political world within which it developed.
4. Discuss the character qualities of the four men—how were they alike or not alike. What does the Bible teach about the character qualities you have discovered?

Just in Time for WWI:

But, it wasn't until after World War I that radio became a normal part of American households.

1. How did WWI affect the development of wireless radio?
2. What specific advances were made in the war years that had an impact on the outcome of the war?

Becoming Part of American Culture:

In 1922, less than 60,000 families owned radios. But, by 1930, only eight years later, over 13 million families owned a radio, connected to the world at large. The information age, as we know it today, was born.

1. Describe what early radios looked like. How many images of vintage radios can you fine online?
2. Where were the major radio manufacturers? Are any of them still in business today?
3. Where were radios manufactured during this time?

Filling the Airwaves:

Radio programs used sound effects and scripts to make their broadcasts seem real, painting detailed pictures in the imaginations of their listeners. The arts, music, drama, comedy, live news coverage, and intelligent conversation filled the airwaves. Radio theatres reached their greatest popularity in the 1930's and 1940's.

1. Where did the talent come from to create the variety of radio shows in the 1930's and 1940's?

2. Where did the money come from to support the costs of producing radio shows?
3. What kinds of advances in radio came about during WWII?
4. How did radio in the WWII years differ in how it was used in the WWI years?

Producing a Radio Show:

In the big broadcasting stations, theatrical stars performed on the radio in front of live studio audiences. Signs flashed telling everyone when they were broadcasting "ON THE AIR." And when they should applaud. The radio theatre stage was full of cumbersome technical equipment and large microphones. Actors read from a script and didn't need to wear costumes. Though, for the studio audience, they might use a special hat or prop in fun. When actors weren't reading their lines in front of the microphone, they'd sit in a chair and wait for their cue. Special Sound Engineers were in charge of creating all the sound effects needed to tell the stories. There were clever ways of making all sorts of sounds.

1. What were some of the clever ways sound engineers produced various sound effects?
2. What is the job of a "film foley" in the movies and how is that similar to an old time sound effect engineer in radio?
3. How much of radio was performed live as opposed to recorded and rerun programs?
4. What were the main broadcast stations of the day? How many were there and are they they still around? How does that compare with the number of radio stations today?
5. Why are we able to have so many radio station choices today?

Radio Show Genres:

Different shows were broadcast with commercial sponsors advertising their products. Educational shows and sporting events were popular and many programs featured Christian preachers teaching about the Bible and faith in God. Family entertainment was very popular—adventure stories, mystery stories, comedy shows, and the exciting serial stories told in short episodes, leaving you with a cliffhanger ending. You'd have to wait until the next episode was broadcast the following week at the same time—or perhaps later on in the day—before you could find out what happened next. You wouldn't want to miss that!

1. What were some of the famous commercial brand sponsors of radio shows?
2. How does the style of radio advertising commercials today differ from the style of advertising in radio's heyday? Why?
3. What were some of the popular radio shows? Who were the big radio stars? What types of programs did people enjoy the most?

4. How did the popularity of certain radio shows impact American culture?

Famous Radio Bands and Singers:

Musicians played instruments in the studio—whole orchestras—and famous singing stars visited, performing their hit songs live and in person.

1. Who were the popular radio stars of the 1930's-1940's? How did their popularity impact American culture?
2. What kind of music was popular at this time? Who were the important bands and where did they play?

Participants in History:

Radio became the common experience uniting millions of Americans—all classes of society and every ethnic group listened to radio. Live broadcasts of important world events and instant access to information made Americans participants in history rather than just observers of history.

1. How did owning a radio unite a nation?
2. How did radio allow people to participate in history making events rather than be passive observers of events?

The Most Famous Radio Drama Broadcast Ever:

Orson Welle's *War of the Worlds* was a watershed moment in radio history. The impact and power to persuade a listening audience that the world was, indeed, being invaded by aliens on that night of October 31, 1938, proved how powerful dramatic storytelling is to captivate minds with the spoken word. Panic ensued in pockets of the nation, tuning in after the broadcast was introduced. People believed the invasion was real! My students were fascinated with some of the accounts of how people reacted at the time. This led to constructive discussion to understand the great responsibility a communicator takes upon himself/herself when they seek to use the power of story through dramatized words.

1. Listen to the War of the Worlds on YouTube.
2. Discuss what you hear in how the play is performed by the actors. What makes them believable?
3. Could the panic this broadcast caused happen today?

You can see, there's plenty of back story study that can lay a strong foundation of understanding in you and your students for producing a radio drama show. Enjoy the journey as you grow together in this creative endeavor.

SCRIPT & ROYALTY FEES

The rights to produce *The Adventures of Marshall Mission: Christmas Takes a Holiday* are available to you via script and royalty contract, and per appropriate fees paid. Written permission must be granted by the author and Pageant Wagon Publishing.

Contact Kathryn Ross at **info@pageantwagonpublishing.com** to request contract and payment via PayPal instructions.

Performance Packages:
~ 1 to 2 performances only w/1 Director Script & 12 Actor Scripts @ $175.
~ 3 to 4 performances only w/1 Director Script & 12 Actor Scripts @ $275.
~ Additional Scripts available @ $8.00 each

For more scripts to bring quality drama with a biblical worldview to your church, school, or community theatre group, visit us online:

www.pageantwagonpublishing.com/drama-scripts

ABOUT THE AUTHOR

Kathryn Ross is a writer, speaker, and dramatist. She filters her love of history, classic literature, drama, and the arts through God's Word, to inform her words. In addition to an extensive resume of writing, directing, and producing theatrical programs for schools, churches, and in community theatre, she ministers literacy and Christian living principles in a variety of venues. Her works inspire young and old to pursue God's goodness and beauty in their lives.

Trained in Principle Approach® Education through the Foundation for American Christian Education, Miss Kathy previously taught in Christian and home school settings. She has written and taught a four-year middle school/high school level curriculum detailing the History of Drama, inspiring a host of her original church and school plays in addition to full choir cantatas. Her books, Bible study curriculum, and dramas are available in the Book Shop on her website at www.pageantwagonpublishing.

She blogs weekly and podcasts monthly at
TheWritersReverie.com and PageantWagonPublishing.com

www.ingramcontent.com/pod-product-compliance
Lightning Source LLC
Chambersburg PA
CBHW081643040426
42449CB00015B/3442
* 9 7 8 0 9 9 1 0 0 7 0 9 7 *